Praise for

Beth Blecker eloquently describes the importance of having a holistic financial plan and how, more often than not, really great financial advice entails far more than discussions about investing. Throughout the pages of *It's Not Just Money, It's Life*, the author showcases the importance of an advisor connecting all aspects a person's financial life and trying to ensure that they all work together. This book is a must read for both financial planners building a career and those planning for their own financial future.

—Suzanne Siracuse, CEO of Suzanne Siracuse
Consulting Services, LLC

Beth Blecker inspires and educates in equal measure. Her writing, like her wisdom, is heartfelt and sincere. Beth's vision for Eastern Planning and her life has succeeded because of her determination, certainly of values, and desire to truly help others. A blueprint for leadership and personal growth, her book is a must-read for all ages.

—Rita Robbins, President and Founder of Affiliated Advisors

Beth Blecker shares valued life and financial lessons everyone can benefit from. This book shows you how a well-educated financial advisor can help you create the retirement plan that fits your life's goals and, more importantly, how to put that plan into action!

—Ed Slott, CPA, retirement expert, author and founder of
IRAHelp.com, and founder of Ed Slott's
Elite IRA Advisor Group^{SM}

It's
NOT
just

money

IT'S
LIFE

It's
NOT
just
money
IT'S
LIFE

BETH BLECKER

Paperback ISBN: 9781737155904
Hardback ISBN: 9781737155911
eBook ISBN: 9781737155928

BUS027030 BUSINESS & ECONOMICS / Finance / Wealth Management
BUS107000 BUSINESS & ECONOMICS / Personal Success
BIO022000 BIOGRAPHY & AUTOBIOGRAPHY / Women

Cover design by Lisa Barbee
Edited by McKell Parsons
Typeset by Kaitlin Barwick

www.EasternPlanning.com

This book is dedicated to Rita Heckler,
who gave this book its name long before
it was ever conceived or written.

Contents

Contents

Foreword

By Bill Good

Founder and Chairman, Bill Good Marketing, Inc.

Beth Blecker has written a different book on financial planning. It is certainly not a "Do It Yourself" treatment on financial planning. Instead, it's a book to help you understand what a specific type of financial planner can do for your life. It's also a great book for financial planners who would like to get even better at what they do.

Over my own forty-plus years in the financial services industry, I have trained thousands of financial advisors in the business side of financial planning. We counsel and sometimes cajole our clients into implementing the systems necessary to spend more time practicing the craft of financial and investment advice and less time managing their businesses.

Over these many years, I have seen many advisors publish books. Many of these books showcase different strategies for accumulating wealth. But I do not recall any with the focus of "It's Not Just Money, It's Life."

By the time you have finished reading, you will understand what a "fiduciary financial planner" does so you can be confident that's who you engage or, if you have one already, you keep them.

Do You Need a Financial Planner? Yes, you do.

As you read Beth's book, she tells stories of people who really needed help. As you read these stories, ask yourself, "Would I know what to do?" Most likely, you would not know what to do any more than you would know what to do if your car starts making funny noises. You do not have the time or know-how to diagnose and then fix a modern auto with its hi-tech systems. Nor do you have the time and skill to navigate the treacherous waters of investments, insurance, tax planning, and all the other eddies and stagnant ponds of today's investment world.

So yes, you need a trusted financial planner for the same reasons you need a trusted mechanic, banker, dentist, primary care physician, family law attorney, accountant or tax preparer, casualty insurance agent, and even a handyperson to fix broken whatevers.

Modern life is complicated. Expert advice steers you away from the potholes, roadblocks, and traffic jams and sometimes keeps you out of the raging fires we have seen too many times this century.

Do You Have a Financial Plan? Probably not.

According to an article in *Financial Advisor Magazine*, "three out of four boomers don't have a written financial plan for retirement. For millennials, 87 percent don't have a plan and 81 percent of

Gen Xers are without a plan. Overall, only 18 percent had a written financial retirement plan in place."[1]

To have a financial plan, you need a planner. (Once again, you cannot go it alone!) To find that planner, you must decide:

1. "Yes, I need a financial planner."
2. And then, for the tough decision, "How will I know I've found the right one?"

I must tell you. You have lucked out because you have Beth's book in your hands right now.

Remember, *It's Not Just Money, It's Life* is not a DIY financial planning book. It's all about what a financial planner does. If you know what one does or should do, you will have a better chance of finding the right one.

An article on CNBC put it this way: "Standing between you and the things you want is one simple thing: a financial plan.[2]"

I would modify that statement slightly, "Standing between you and the things you want are two simple things: A financial plan and a financial planner who will not only craft the plan to get you from here to there but who will help you get it done."

You will enjoy this book, and it will possibly save your financial life.

1. Jacqueline Sergeant, "Why Most Americans Lack a Written Financial Retirement Plan," *Financial Advisor*, April 23, 2019, https://www.fa-mag.com/news/most-americans-don-t-have-a-written-financial-retirement-plan-44471.html.
2. Jill Cornfield, "Standing between You and the Things You Want Is One Simple Thing. A Financial Plan," *CNBC*, November 5, 2019, https://www.cnbc.com/2019/11/05/people-who-have-their-finances-figured-out-do-this-one-simple-thing.html.

Acknowledgments

I am so grateful for the help, encouragement, and coaching I received from Rob Brown of TruestFan.com. Rob helped me turn an idea into action. Without him, I never could have completed this project.

About Eastern Planning, Inc.

Eastern Planning, Inc. began in 1995 with a simple vision: provide superior customer service and personal, practical advice. In 2000, Beth Blecker took over as CEO of the company and grew the firm to its present scope, serving hundreds of clients nationwide.

We believe very few advisors can match our knowledge and expertise in the areas of retirement planning and distribution strategies, particularly how best to integrate the compensation packages provided to corporate executives at the major firms in our area. Clients appreciate our emphasis on big-picture strategic planning. We don't believe in a once-and-done approach resulting in a written document that sits on a shelf gathering dust. Our clients see their plans almost as a living, breathing resource, designed to change and adapt to whatever happens in their lives.

Eastern Planning is always here to assist our clients in making some of the most important financial decisions with confidence so they can enjoy their lives.

Learn more at EasternPlanning.com.

Introduction

Welcome! I'm so glad you picked up this book. My name is Beth Blecker, and my goal in writing this is to share with you what I do with Eastern Planning, my fiduciary company, and why it's so important to me. In this book, I structured my story around nine lessons I've learned over the years—lessons I hope will be beneficial to you. But before we get into my story, allow me to explain three aspects that underpin the philosophy of this book's title: *it's not just money; it's life.*

First, on a superficial level, this book contains valuable information about financial planning. I'm not writing this as specific financial advice for anyone; that's not how it works, especially not at Eastern Planning! Our work isn't about cookie-cutter plans and systems; it's about tailoring our financial plans to meet the needs of each individual. So I've included stories and observations from my time in the field that should help you better understand our approach to financial planning and, most importantly, what you should look for in a financial planner. My goal is to demonstrate why it's so important to focus on our

tagline—it's not just money; it's life—and why you should seek
the best avenue for success and happiness in life through your
financial planning. In that sense, this book offers a ground-level
look at my work with Eastern Planning.

Second, this book has elements of our methods and philosophies that may be suitable for advising other financial planners and advisors. Again, I'm not trying to provide step-by-step
instructions or a checklist. In fact, that's the whole point! I'm
hoping to show that what we do at Eastern Planning is predicated
on individual people and families: on their lives, expectations,
hopes, hobbies, and visions of the future they want. If you are in
a position to advise others on their financial planning, I hope you
consider taking a more comprehensive approach rather than just a
standard one-size-fits-all plan.

Third, this book also contains personal anecdotes and observations about my life and career. Mostly, I've focused on my philosophy and values, which together were shaped by my personal experiences in the field over several decades of work. As I mentioned,
I didn't expect or plan to become a "female business leader." I was
just a hardworking entrepreneur who learned a lot by handling
life's setbacks and opportunities as they came. In offering tidbits
from my own personal experiences, I want to convey the mindset that life planning—not just financial planning—is a powerful
avenue to adaptable and lasting success.

These three aspects of my work define the fundamental drive
behind Eastern Planning. We're not just about growing financial
security; we're about helping people live lives that make them
happy—and I hope that this book will help you do the same.

Lesson #1

A Plan Isn't a Plan If You Don't Properly Put It into Action

I've always believed money should serve your life, not the other way around. My clients are people who have lives, not just accounts that need managing. After all, what's the point of having money if you can't enjoy yourself?

I started out as a first-grade teacher, largely due to my mother's input—she recommended that I teach so I could be home with my children whenever they were out of school. However, after just one year of subbing and trying to get a full-time position, I decided to find out what I was *truly* destined to be. I went to a career counselor for testing, and lo and behold, I was told I should go into finance. Afterward, I took a job as a bookkeeper while going back to school to study accounting. Once I began work as an accountant, I was constantly dealing with peoples' pasts—financial decisions they had already made—and seeing them struggle to plan for their futures. Being an accountant, I didn't have the freedom to get deeply involved with clients' personal lives, but I yearned to help them. It is this passion for people that drove me toward financial planning: I wanted to help people manage their lives, not just their money.

That was the start of Eastern Planning.

To help people reach their goals and objectives to have a wonderful future, my ex-husband, Alan, and I established our financial planning business, Eastern Planning. We'd get a client, talk with them about their financial needs, strategize, and send them off with a plan to implement it. Six months later, we'd meet again to see how things were working for them. It rarely went well. Some people set up everything we planned; however, many others did not. Sometimes, life simply got in the way. Other times, another financial professional would sell them a product other than what we had planned. Stockbrokers and insurance agents were the biggest offenders, often off-setting well-laid plans to benefit their company's bottom line. No matter the reason, something had gone wrong. Plans don't work if you don't follow them—and if you don't continuously update them as life continually happens.

We needed a better solution.

In 1995, I dealt with two clients who were prime examples of this disconnect. We were working with a couple in their early thirties who had three children under the age of five. The mother wasn't working, but she planned to go back to her career in a few years. The father was a corporate executive who made very good money. One of my concerns was their lack of savings, but they wouldn't be able to save much until their youngest child was old enough to start daycare and the mother could go back to work.

My biggest concern was that this family didn't have any life insurance, except for what the father's company provided, which was three times his salary. That seemed like a lot of money to the couple, but it wouldn't cover all the family's needs if the father were suddenly not there to support them. They could squeak by on three years' worth of benefit, but what they really needed was *lifetime* planning—something to support a family of their size for a significant period. I decided to create a plan that would protect the family if something happened to either parent.

I recommended a twenty-five-year term policy for the husband with a $2,000,000 death benefit. That might seem excessive, but the youngest child was only a year old, and they wanted the plan to cover the youngest child's college education in a worst-case scenario. Due to this, I also included a twenty-five-year term policy with a $500,000 death benefit for the mother. If she died, her husband would need to hire help so he could continue to provide for the family. The clients reviewed the plan and agreed to the need for more coverage, but their insurance agent told them it was a waste of money.

From an insurance standpoint, it makes sense when you think about it; term insurance doesn't pay the agent much of a commission. The agent would likely make a bigger commission—even on a smaller policy—if this family bought whole life insurance. That's exactly what happened. The agent sold them a $50,000 whole-life policy for the husband and a $25,000 policy for the wife. When the couple came back for their six-month review, they were very proud of themselves. They had actually moved forward on their plan. They bought life insurance.

It fell on us to then inform them of the results of their permanent insurance purchase. Alan and I had to bluntly tell them, "If you die tomorrow, what's $50,000 going to do for your family? It won't even pay for a year's worth of expenses. Isn't it worth it to pay an insurance company a smaller amount of money over twenty-five years to guarantee your children are going to be taken care of?" We had to treat it like auto and homeowner's insurance: we hoped they would never need it, but we knew they would be glad they had it if anything disastrous ever happened to their family.

For us, that was the straw that broke the camel's back. I realized that although we might have a great plan, our clients didn't have an obligation to put it into motion. No matter how great it was, I couldn't send people off to implement it on their own. A financial plan is a tool that needs to be put into action. Without that action, it's just a fancy piece of paper with complicated charts. It's like a book without a plot: it won't give the client the help they sorely need.

What does that piece of paper mean to a family that has lost someone? This was my primary concern. For instance, I wanted to make sure this couple had a plan that would remove any additional barriers if something happened to either parent. Instead, they were sold something that would likely increase their anxiety and make their lives even harder if either spouse had to run a single-parent household.

As a financial advisor, it was my responsibility to plan *with* our clients. We decided it was time to move away from just giving advice and become an independent financial advisor who could help implement the ideas we recommended; that's why we started Eastern Planning.

My team and I would sit down with people, learn about their lives and their current and future needs, and develop a plan that suited their most important goals and challenges. I could work on the implementation of the plans *we* were creating *with* my clients. As life happened and changes became necessary, we could then modify their financial plans to reflect new goals and realities. Unlike many other financial advisors and companies, we realized circumstances change over time and, as such, our clients' financial plans should change accordingly.

My experiences had shown that I wasn't content to just formulate a plan and send clients on their way. I wanted them to actually succeed by (1) putting a plan into action and (2) making the best use of their money, time, and resources.

In short, I wanted my planning and assistance to be effective—and I knew that wouldn't happen unless I were more closely involved with my clients. I had to help them over time to develop plans that could change, grow, and adapt to their circumstances. In time, that became the framework of what Eastern Planning is today.

What a relief! I knew I had found my calling as a financial professional. Sure, it had taken me almost twenty years to go from bookkeeper to accountant to financial planner to trusted financial advisor, but I knew I could serve my clients better than ever.

I worked this way on my own for a while and was lucky to have my son, Matthew, join me in the firm when Alan and I split. Gradually, Matthew and I realized we could do even more to care for our clients. We couldn't just be concerned with numbers; it was never about the numbers for me. It was always about serving people. We weren't just managing money; financial planning isn't just about growing financial security—it's about people living lives that make them happy.

We rededicated ourselves to serve the whole person—a human being with challenges, hopes, and dreams, who wanted our help to make sure they could meet those needs and fulfill those dreams over a lifetime, and even beyond, in terms of their family legacies. After all, people are more than their net worth.

Lesson #2

~~~

Good Planning Leads to a More Enjoyable Life

In coming to the realization that people are at the center of financial planning and then developing our business to make that our focus, I've learned something very valuable about human nature.

You see, the biggest fear most people hold deep inside is that of having more life than money. Generally speaking, that fear uncovers two types of people: spenders and savers. First, we have people who could run out of money if they don't know when to stop spending. They have probably spent years consuming too much and saving too little. Now that they are retired, they need to live on a smaller pool of savings and investments than they need to maintain their lifestyles. They need help to understand their limits and to live within their means.

Fortunately, most of our clients are savers. They have spent years spending less and saving more. That's how they've gotten where they are, and that's why they have us help manage their financial lives. They need to live the retirement of their dreams.

Eventually, they reach a point when it's time to spend and not save, to enjoy and not accumulate, but it's really hard for them to shift their mindset. And that's a good problem to have!

One of the stories I tell everyone who walks in the door is about a client who was planning her first flight by herself to visit her son in Israel. Let's call her Ann. A few years earlier, she and her husband had just begun their well-planned retirement when her husband unexpectedly passed away. The two of them had worked hard and lived a modest life, which together led to financial security for their retirement. Her husband passed just as they were starting the next stage, and Ann's life changed drastically from what she had always expected. Even though she had enough assets to maintain her lifestyle and comfort for the rest of her life—and still leave plenty to her children when she passed—Ann was terribly (and understandably) worried about making this long international trip by herself.

When Ann came to meet with me, she was both excited and nervous. Her greatest worry in planning the trip was the actual flight. She had flown internationally before, but always with her husband and always in coach—and she never liked it. Now, she would be traveling alone, and she felt like she needed to skimp on her plane flight. I asked Ann why she didn't want to fly first-class. Her response? "I'm not rich! I can't afford first-class!"

I was puzzled. Why didn't Ann think she was rich? She had always saved her money and lived below her means. She also had plenty of money set aside for precisely this sort of situation—for a period of retirement in which she could use her savings without worry, maybe even to indulge. However, because she had spent her whole life working hard and living modestly, she initially had a hard time seeing it that way. To use her money now, for the kind of travel she had dreamed about to see her son, was not easy for her to accept.

Oftentimes, people who save find it extremely hard to spend their money, even if it is not the principal but the growth and income they have accumulated over time. For these people, we are here to help them spend without worrying about overspending. After all, they would probably never end up overspending because it just isn't in their nature to begin with. Our job is to help our clients plan with confidence and enjoy life. In this case, my response was, "Of course you can fly first-class! Of course you can afford it." Ann ended up taking the first-class flight to see her son, and she thanked me for my help in making it happen, She told me it was something she would never forget.

In the process, I *also* learned more about my own role in helping my clients. I realized I was there to help them spend their money, not overspend it. It was my job to help my clients plan with confidence so that they could enjoy life.

Through years of this type of planning, I've met many, many people who did not know they can do things to enjoy their lives more fully. Sometimes we get caught up in the stresses and milestones of life and forget to slow down. I've had clients who needed both education and encouragement to understand the reality of their financial situation. Once they understood their situation, they could make decisions in line with their goals and priorities.

My daughter, Jacklyn, offers a good example of balancing spending and saving. Both of my children have become amazing individuals and powerful in their own rights. I talk more about Matthew later, but Jacklyn deserves a shout-out of her own. One of the greatest joys of life is to see your children become the people you hoped they would be, and my children became even more so.

Although my daughter has always been the person who wanted to achieve as much as she could, she inherited some learning disabilities from me. I have a mild case of something—not quite dyslexia—and to this day I type P instead of a B, and I can't add or subtract in my head at all. Don't ask me to do multiplication tables either. I still use my fingers! Thank God for calculators, so I don't have to do it myself!

I never thought I would go into a career with numbers, but thank goodness Matthew became my business partner. He's a math whiz—has been since he was a little boy. He truly has a gift for numbers. Unfortunately, Jacklyn takes after me. Throughout her life, I always worked with her so that she would succeed. Neither of us can spell, so on the morning of a spelling test, we would memorize spelling words by singing songs. At night, as we would head to her room to study, we'd pass by Matthew lying on his bed with a book on his stomach, and Jacklyn would say, "Oh look! Matt is studying again."

Jacklyn and I worked together through her youth, and eventually her hard work and diligence paid off. She graduated high school in the top three of her class. All three spoke at graduation, and although they didn't specifically rank them in order, in my mind my daughter was always number one.

Then she went off to college. How many mothers call up their daughters and tell them to stop studying because they've studied enough? I had to do that. I would call Jacklyn and say, "You've studied enough. Go out. You can go to the sorority dance or your sorority meeting. It's okay. You've studied enough."

That's who she is. That's how she's always been. That's the balance of her life, but she had to work to balance her ambition and accomplishments (and maybe take a few of those friendly phone calls from Mom along the way). Jacklyn always worked so hard, just like some of my clients who save and save and never take the time to enjoy the fruits of their hard work.

Just like I had to remind Jacklyn every so often to stop studying and go out to enjoy her life, I work with my clients to help them understand their goals, ambitions, and livelihoods. That's why we develop plans for them that *make sense* with what and who they want to be. We're not all about just saving money, because that's not what life is all about. You have to live your life. You have to know when you've saved enough and when it's time to go out and spend a little.

In Jacklyn's case, her hard work and saving paid off. Her life is *full* of living right now. She has three children; she's a corporate executive; she has a beautiful home, a lovely husband, and a wonderful marriage. Plus, she's balanced. She's learned how to save and how to spend, and she's used her plans to make her life the one she wants to live. It took her a while to learn this, just like it sometimes takes my clients a while to get used to the idea that they can actually spend some of their savings!

Many people prepare for retirement by saving, saving, saving. Despite their preparation, they worry so much about running out of money that they wind up not enjoying the rest of their lives. That's one of my biggest goals for my clients: to let them know they can absolutely enjoy their lives within the scope of their financial plans. They can really *live* and remain fiscally secure.

Trust me, that isn't always a one-time explanation. Sometimes my clients need to be reminded repeatedly of the opportunities that exist within their plans. Remember the client I mentioned earlier? Even though Ann flew first-class and raved about the flight after she returned, when it was time to book her flight to see her son in Israel again, I received a phone call and she asked, "Do I have enough money to fly first-class again this year?" Some habits are not easily broken.

This reminds me of another client—let's call her Sarah. Like so many great savers, Sarah was always afraid she would spend too much money. Her fear, in large part, came from being a single, divorced woman.

One day, somewhat out of character for her, Sarah came to me and said, "I want to go on vacation with my entire family. I'm getting older, and I want to celebrate my seventy-fifth birthday." As is often the case, it was hard to get her adult children and her overscheduled grandchildren together. Plus, she didn't want them to have to spend money they could be saving to celebrate her birthday. So I said to her, "Give yourself a present and pay for a cruise. Take your whole family on the cruise."

As expected, her response was, "Oh, I don't have enough money. How can I do that?" I had worked with her on her budget and knew her cashflow and lifestyle. I replied, "You have a certain amount of money you can spend every single month. You never spend it, so you wind up saving it. When we have our meetings, you always have more and more in your savings account. You have enough money in your savings account to pay for this cruise without touching your investments. Do it!"

She did. When Sarah and her family got back from the cruise, she said it was the best birthday present she had ever had—and she gave it to herself. She couldn't remember the last time she had experienced so much fun and spent so much time with her family. Because of her planning, she was in an awesome financial position. She just needed some reassurance and encouragement to live a little without the fear of jeopardizing her financial security. That fear was understandable; no one wants to feel like they need to go to their children to ask for financial help. However, the opposite extreme—saving everything and never enjoying the fruit of your hard work—isn't a pleasant way to live, either.

As a financial advisor, my role is often to be a coach, someone who can tell you when you're on the right track and when you're not. Someone you can count on to tell you both, "Yes, it's okay to fly first-class" or "Whoa, hang on! Not another cruise just now." Of course, it doesn't have to be so black and white. Many people think it's a choice between vanilla and chocolate: spend your money or save it; live luxuriously or be prudent and modest. In reality, there are many other flavors of ice cream, just as there are many other options and choices in retirement. Finance is a gray area with various shades, different choices, and abundant options—and all of them are available to our clients! The problem is that sometimes they don't know what those alternatives are or how they may affect them over time. They might not be in a position to properly evaluate their choices or consider all the ramifications.

That's our job as financial advisors. We lay out the possibilities, and then we help our clients take the opportunity to make better decisions for their lives.

Some of my clients say I give them permission, but what I feel I am doing is showing them where they are and where they could be if they make certain decisions. I help them look at all the prospects and explore the consequences. I'm just a guide, offering a helpful perspective to inform the decisions they will make. "Look, you could do this; this is an option. If you do that, then this might happen. Or you can stay and do it this way, but then look what could potentially happen." Then they have an opportunity to make better, more informed decisions.

That's why I'm so proud of what we've built at Eastern Planning. Too few financial advisory firms help their clients understand how to invest and spend their money so they can truly enjoy their lives. We care about our clients and their families, and that makes a difference to them in more ways than could possibly be measured on a spreadsheet. The privilege of serving my clients this way makes a difference in *my* life because I feel I'm doing something that's absolutely worthwhile.

This really is a life-changing work for everyone involved. The more people we can serve, the more we can also serve their families, and the more we're going to make a difference in the world. Instead of just investing for investing's sake, more people will understand the power of their money and live their lives to the fullest.

One of the reasons we focus so heavily on long-term life planning is because I understand firsthand how situations can change and difficulties can arise unexpectedly. Even Eastern Planning, in its current incarnation, is the result of a transformation and a lot of hard work that followed a particularly difficult life and business event for me. That experience, which I'll explain shortly, helped me understand that planning for success in *life* rather than just in finances is key to true satisfaction. Even the best-laid plans can go astray, but we've found—through our own sometimes tumultuous history—that considering the whole picture for our clients is the best way for us to help them.

Someone once told me that being a financial planner is like being a pilot. If someone wants to fly to Hawaii, then they buy a ticket, get on the plane, and expect to land in Hawaii. The pilot uses all their skill to get their passengers there safely. Storms might come up, mechanical difficulties might come up, and the route might be changed, but in the end, the passengers land in Hawaii.

Likewise, as financial planners, we use our skills to help you get where you want to go. No matter what storms come up, we suggest the course changes that help you live the life you want.

I do this work because it's who I am. I'm a mother, teacher, and caregiver. For me, working with my clients and seeing them have lives they love is very satisfying. I feel extremely rewarded for helping them and seeing their lives work.

It's not just my income. It's not just my business. It's my life—and I want you to have the same satisfaction in your life.

Lesson #3

No Plan Is Perfect. Always Be Prepared to Make Difficult Decisions

In my work with clients, I help them make plans for their future, but I also help them adjust when life happens and circumstances change. Like so many people, I've experienced my own unexpected changes and difficulties—especially when it came to starting, growing, and adapting my business.

Our Beginnings

When Eastern Planning was started in 1995, I was a co-owner with our lead financial advisor: my husband, Alan. As we grew Eastern Planning, no matter how hard I worked or what I accomplished, I never quite felt satisfied. Then one day, as I sat talking to a client waiting to go into his session with Alan, it hit me: what I was missing was being with clients on the front line, rather than hiding in the background. Right then and there, I made a promise to myself that I was going to get educated and start seeing clients on my own. I knew it wasn't going to be easy. I knew I would make mistakes, but it didn't matter. I was 100 percent up for the challenge and ready to dive in head first. Over the next five years, I educated myself on many aspects of financial planning, developed my skills in working with people, and became a full-on financial advisor. Things were moving fast, and I was falling in love with the idea of serving our clients.

At the same time, I realized there were a lot of things happening at Eastern Planning I didn't like. In many ways, I also started feeling as though I was there to run the business administratively—that I was being taken for granted and not utilizing my hard-won skills and talents. That caused major issues at work and at home. Alan and I decided it would be best to split the business, but that didn't resolve all the challenges. Unfortunately, we split up personally as well. Since Alan was the lead advisor, he took most of the clients. That was scary. As I now discuss with all my clients, I wanted to be in control of my expenses.

A theme you will hear throughout this book is there are two types of people: the spenders and the savers. The spenders usually come up with good reasons for spending more than they should, while the savers usually have to be pushed into spending anything extra and enjoying what they have accumulated. As I write this, I realize there is another category, and that is where I fit: sort of in-between. Sometimes I will spend a little too much, but most times I try to stay within the guidelines of my personal financial plan. That was a big problem in my business relationship with Alan. He believed in a large overhead—the more employees and the more stuff, the better. If he spent more, he could build more. He just hoped the clients would come and didn't worry about what would happen if they didn't.

Also, and I hate to admit this, our business wasn't very client-centric, which it should have been. Although he cared for his clients, I believed Alan was more product driven. Realizing that difference has led to another awareness about proper financial planning and the work I have done since.

The differences in our fundamental approaches were clear. Staying with the status quo was no longer an option. Once the decision was made, it was up to me to make the plan work. This was a painful, expensive process and a big risk for me to take at that time in my life. Like the title of this book, it wasn't just my money (or even my marriage)—it was my life. I wanted to live a life I loved and run a business helping other people live lives they love too.

∽ New Beginnings ∽

Rebuilding Eastern Planning in 2001 was incredibly difficult. After the breakup, my personal finances were extremely stressed, leaving me to build my own financial security while trying to navigate this huge change in our business approach. Like most young businesses, Eastern Planning took several years to become financially stable. As an entrepreneur, you don't get big bank loans—and that was especially the case in those days. You do whatever it takes to fund your business, and that's exactly what I did, including downsizing my house. I look back now and I'm *amazed* that I was able to move from where I was in 2001 to where I am today.

When Alan left, I found myself with most of the expenses and debt of our business—and with less than half of the clients! I had to work awfully hard to rebuild and expand, and that involved some unconventional choices and some serious effort. I experienced major difficulties with bank loans, trying to manage staff and overhead, and rebuilding a workable client base and business model. Over time, I managed to recover many of the clients I'd lost, and later on, we grew Eastern Planning into something grand that I never imagined it could be.

I don't share this looking for praise or pity but just to demonstrate that I have personal experience with how immense life's challenges can be and how quickly plans can fall apart. Thankfully, the work I put into rebuilding Eastern Planning proved profitable, not only for myself and my team but also for all our clients and their families. Those experiences have truly reinforced the importance of our methods in helping clients plan for their future, whatever that may hold.

On that topic, when I found myself at the helm of Eastern Planning and had to figure out how to make a new beginning, I realized that we were not just changing how we handled clients—our entire business model needed updating. Luckily, while all of this was happening in 2001, my son, Matthew, joined me fresh out of college with a business degree. He took a lot of the burden off my shoulders during a really tough time.

Having Matthew join my business at this time was huge, but I was also blessed by the total and complete support I received from my daughter. Jacklyn's influence was what enabled me to trudge on. She was my sounding board and my cheerleader. As an assignment for one of her courses in school, she helped me prepare the first Eastern Planning business plan. Jacklyn's and Matthew's help truly made all the difference.

My son and I transitioned our clients from a commission-based model into a fee-based model that allowed all of us to sit on the same side of the table. We always placed their interests at heart, not financial products. I was happy with our new focus and the new direction we were moving. I felt we were helping people make plans that would truly impact their lives beyond the details of their spending and saving. However, it was a challenge to transition into a fee-based model, and that switch came with unforeseen complications and hazards. That transition became even more difficult after the tragedy of 9/11 in 2001 and the huge market turndown.

The tragedy of that day was immediate and personal for us. We lived and worked very close to New York City, and many of our clients either worked in the city or had family and friends who lived there. As a result, my thoughts immediately turned to their safety and well-being. When our phones were finally back up and running, my first response was to call clients and make sure they and their families were safe at home. It was a terribly frightening environment, and I could see firsthand the unfolding devastation. The Twin Towers were prominent during my work and travel, and my daughter's dormitory was right next to the White House, so the news of the tragedy in Washington, DC, was another heart-breaking event. It was horrifying how many people we dealt with who had immediate family and friends involved in the tragedy. Many people were traumatized on every level—and, of course, so was the financial environment.

The events of 9/11 severely impacted the financial world in the United States. Despite our worries about the ongoing success of our work and our clients, we persevered with our new model and our new approach to helping people. In hindsight, we realize it was a phenomenal undertaking and accomplishment. From that time on, no matter how we were doing personally, we never went back to the old way of doing business. Matthew helped us stand firm. I was extremely worried about finances (and we were definitely a little shaky), but he helped us keep things moving the way we wanted. We stuck with our new model. We became a fiduciary firm, acting for our clients, not just with them. The tragedy of 9/11 had tested our goal to focus on the lives of our clients and not just their money. Even with everything else that happened, our purpose was tremendously satisfying to us and to our clients, so we carried on and never went back.

As I mentioned, my son was invaluable during this time. Matthew decided to join Eastern Planning after graduating from Penn State. His presence and contributions to Eastern Planning were especially critical in handling the personal, business, and financial aftermath of that tragedy—not to mention all the rebranding we were doing with the business.

A more natural choice for Matthew would have been to take a job on Wall Street. He'd just finished up in college and wanted to go into the investment business, so Wall Street would have been a smooth transition for him. I know many of his friends from school did just that. However, for Matthew, the idea of a family business had always been more appealing. He'd spent a lot of time working with us already, and he enjoyed the idea of a flexible work schedule and a more personalized approach to business and life. More than that, he recognized what I was going through after my husband and I separated.

For him, the risk of joining Eastern Planning was worth it to help me out and to pursue something that seemed a better fit for his personality and tastes than Wall Street would have been. His rationale was that if this didn't work out, it would only mean a delay of a few years before he got a more stable position at a bigger firm. But at least by trying his hand at this new venture, he would know if it was something he wanted to spend his life doing. He recognized it was a risk he could take and that it would be worth it in the end.

We've intrinsically had our fair share of bumps along the road, but Matthew agrees our work together has largely been the right choice for both of us. He initially studied corporate finance in school but eventually decided to focus on individual portfolio construction and concentrate in areas related to financial planning, such as tax strategies, estates and trusts, insurance, and pension plan rules. He was able to capitalize on that background when he joined Eastern Planning, and his knowledge helped us immensely.

A look at the evolution of my work and Eastern Planning's responses to distinct challenges demonstrates the principles of life planning that this book is all about. So let me explain how my ventures into the world of financial planning began.

Initially, Alan and I charged a fee for some of our accounting and financial planning services. Alan was a CPA, and I worked on operations and books. When he earned his CFP license, we shifted into full-time financial planning, but we never worked directly on investment management; we always outsourced it to other firms. Over time, our planning work evolved into developing plans for clients and then sending them to different professionals for help implementing the plan.

Even when we transitioned into full financial planning, we never had the same expertise in investment management that we did in other areas, so we always used third-party money managers or outsourced that work to other wholesalers or professionals. As I mentioned, our approach did not work as smoothly as we wanted, and we ended up divorcing and separating our business.

Alan, who was more sales oriented, left for Florida and took some of the larger clients with him, leaving me at Eastern Planning with our smaller clients and most of the overhead and expenses. I had a frank conversation with Matthew, who by then was well-qualified to offer advice and suggestions about the best way forward. We discussed whether we should close Eastern Planning and go out to take other jobs—or try making it work with the infrastructure we still had, despite the expenses and limited client base and everything else going on. Together, we decided to give it a shot.

We had to rebuild a client base. I focused on marketing, elder care and estate planning, and total comprehensive, holistic financial planning, while Matthew developed his understanding of investment management enough to produce our own portfolios. He then expanded his expertise to include tax planning, beneficiary designation, and a host of other aspects of setting up managed accounts for clients.

Remember, this was happening shortly after 9/11, and we had to rely on making positive connections with our clients and building strong relationships. We didn't have the luxury of relying on our previous methods of obtaining clients. Instead, we had to work hard to transition into a referral-style business to become profitable again. That meant reaching out to our clients and establishing trust with them, and from those experiences our tagline was born: *it's not just money; it's life*.

We were certainly far from being the hardest hit by 9/11. Still, those events and the following deterioration of the financial status quo proved to be a crucible and a catalyst for Eastern Planning. Thanks to Matthew's close involvement and our requisite focus on establishing trustworthy relationships with clients, we transformed our business into something that makes actual, meaningful change in people's lives.

That first year, following 9/11 and the technology bubble and everything that happened, was incredibly challenging. It was something I never could have planned for. Yet I learned how to adjust my plans, respond to events in my life, focus on money as just one important aspect of my life, and build a profitable and outward-focused business by truly serving clients and their needs.

This period led to a new beginning—for me, for Matthew, and for Eastern Planning. Since then, we have continued to work to provide similar new beginnings for all our clients.

ᥒ Building a Woman-Led Business ᥒ

Sometimes, you don't fully appreciate all the things you have done until they're in the rearview mirror. I now realize what I did in 2001 was unusual—not giving up after my divorce or going out to get another job but starting my own business, taking over the reins of Eastern Planning, and building it into my vision, and doing so as a woman in the male-dominated financial service industry. My role as a female entrepreneur never really occurred to me. Owning and running a client-focused business was just something I knew I needed and desired to do.

Everything we did was based on pure determination and the belief that what we were doing was helpful and necessary to the clients we would be fortunate to serve. I never said, "I'm going to be a female business leader. Isn't that wonderful?" I never even thought about the words "female business leader." However, looking back, we had to make sure people understood who I was, what I did, what I could do, and that I was up to the task at hand.

One of our challenges was finding a new strategic partner to help us facilitate our business and act as our back office. As soon as Alan left, it was like I was a distant second cousin to our former strategic partner. They didn't see me as a worthwhile business owner. They thought I would be the work-from-home part-timer who didn't contribute nearly enough, making me unprofitable to them.

Fortunately for me, an old associate of mine called me just to see how I was doing. She was a female regional manager who had switched from our former strategic partner to a new firm. She had a reasonably good understanding of who I was and what my business could become. I told her, "What perfect timing! I was just looking into changing strategic partners, and your new firm is on my list." Our newly formed strategic relationship made what came next so much easier. Her firm knew Eastern Planning was under new leadership, and they genuinely wanted to do business with us. That relationship proved valuable for both parties. For years, they have ranked us in the top fifty of all their strategic alliances. Our partnership has certainly been mutually beneficial.

Next, there were staffing changes to tackle. I helped build the team in 1995, so I knew Eastern Planning had some wonderful people. Sadly, the company was too big. As I mentioned, Alan believed bigger was better. Why just hire one person for a job when you could have two? If I felt we needed a team of four, he insisted on a team of ten—expenses were not an issue for him. But Eastern Planning was not made of money. There were people on our team who had no idea what they contributed. Worse, I didn't know either.

The more salaries, the more titles, the more people he had under him, the more powerful Alan felt. Now that I was in charge, that meant I had to decide who to fire. Firing staff is not something I do well, even now, nineteen years later. Rightsizing the team was terribly difficult to do. I had to cut the number of staff we had to less than half—a daunting task, especially considering all the other changes we were making and the challenges I knew lay ahead.

Everyone I let go was eligible for unemployment, so my unemployment insurance expenses were unusually high for several years. This was happening just as we were building the business back up and didn't have a lot of extra cash on hand. But it was crucial to build an efficient, friendly team that could do what I needed them to do as we restructured our business model and worked to give our clients the care and attention they deserved.

In those early days, I realized I wanted client input in the company and made a client board of directors, a place where I could ask for help with moving my business forward and developing an ideal version of Eastern Planning that worked both for me and for my clients. We had several meetings to discuss various topics like color themes, stationery, mission statements, and all the other important minutiae of establishing ourselves anew. We didn't always agree, but we found more common ground than I had expected, and both sides benefited.

During one of these meetings, one of our clients officially gave us our tagline. She had referred many people to us, and I said, "It's almost like you're a salesperson for my office! I don't know how to thank you." That's when she replied, "I need to thank *you*, and I need to share it with everybody I know. Because you made me realize it's not just my money; it's my *life*. And you help me enjoy my life." I realized *that* had to be Eastern Planning's tagline. That's who we are. *It's not just money; it's life.*

Unfortunately, this client developed lung cancer and died at a relatively young age. She was an important figure in my life, and I am glad I helped her enjoy the years she had in retirement. I was proud to know and serve her while I could but was equally saddened to see her go. She was a building block during our developmental days, and without her insight, Eastern Planning would not be the same business it is today.

This book is dedicated to her, and Eastern Planning is also dedicated to her philosophy: *"It's not just money; it's life."*

$\mathcal{L}esson$ #4

~~~

Tell It All! Good Planning Starts with Detailed Information

Back in 2001, one of the most important things we had to master was discerning who to work with. There's nothing worse than a company that tries to be everything for everyone, and we knew it. The question then arose, "Who should we be serving?"

Potential clients who would ask us to manage their accounts without showing us the whole picture—who they were, where they were, and what their goals were—weren't a good fit for us. We weren't account managers. We preferred to work with our clients to meet specific goals and to overcome challenges. Not only were long-term relationships more profitable, but they also allowed us to follow clients through their journey and to see how our recommendations turned out. Sure, when we first meet, they fill out the data form we give them. However, they also tell us about their son, their grandchildren, their daughter, and their future son-in-law (whom they're not sure they like). They tell us about vacation homes they have or desire to own, trips they want to take, and charities they want to support. We don't have to push ourselves on our clients. Our clients are the ones who hire us because they know they want more than just a money manager. They, too, come to believe "it's not just money; it's life!"

We are also not a good fit for people who are only looking to the next year or even the next five years. Sure, those can be important timeframes, but limiting your planning to shorter periods of time often ignores or even takes away from the things that matter most in the long haul. That kind of short-term thinking is what Wayne Gretzky denounced when he said, "Go to where the puck is going, not where it has been." We want to work with clients who are interested not only in short-term gain but also in living the rest of their lives—financial and beyond.

When people call and ask for an appointment—often because someone referred them to us—we send them a data form to fill out and ask them to bring it with them to our first meeting. We ask them to complete it as fully as they can but not to worry if they don't know how to answer every question. We also ask them to bring in their investment, savings, and retirement plan statements, along with any other important financial information. The people who come best prepared for this fact-gathering meeting are typically the clients with whom we work best. Those who choose not to fully engage in the process may just be dipping their toes in the water. They may not really want to participate in the full scope of our services, which means we probably won't be a good fit for each other.

When I sit with a prospective client, the first things I ask them are, "Why now? What brought you here? What do you hope to accomplish?"

Experience tells me something has prompted that person to take action, and I want to know exactly what that nudge might have been. Quite often it's a life event. Either something has recently happened in their life that they're responding to or a future milestone is fast approaching. Almost always, part of the reason they're coming to see me is because they have an immense pile of money in their retirement plans and company stock, but they never really took the time to manage it. They haven't been educated—the potential client doesn't *really* know what's going on inside of their financial planning, and they crave additional information and assurance. If I can get them to talk, to totally open up, to explain their complete situation, to tell me the reasons they're not happy or concerned, to tell me what they really want out of life (even if things aren't exactly where they need to be), then it's the beginning of a beautiful relationship.

༄ Expecting the Unexpected ༄

As much as we try to get to know our new clients as well as we can, sometimes we're surprised by what we learn as they share their lives with us. We keep our radar up and stay ready to plan for things we never expect.

For example, if I'm speaking with a client and they offhandedly mention their concern about their parents, I ask more. It's up to me to find out if the parent hasn't given them the power of attorney yet. Or if they have no idea what their parents' finances are. Or if they don't know how the parents are going to afford to take care of themselves. Now I can offer to help with something that could have major financial repercussions in their lives, even if they didn't think to mention it. Caring about how their lives are going is important!

If we don't talk to our clients about their parents while the parents can be involved, we might end up helping our clients try to sort through their parents' assets that are spread all over the place. For instance, when a client's mother passed away, she had several millions of dollars of stock to be split between the daughters. The problem was they were not in a brokerage house; they were held at each company. We tried to gather up all the stock certificates and get them into the trust the mother had, but we were not able to account for all of them.

Over the next several months, we had to track down the stocks that were either still paying dividends or, at tax time, sent out as a 1099. It was time-consuming, difficult work for the daughters. There was one stock certificate that was not put into the trust, and we had to have an estate attorney probate the estate just for that one stock. Thinking ahead can sometimes save a lot of time and money.

Occasionally, our clients run into other problems too. When a parent dies, it can be too late to help get things organized, so Eastern Planning helps before that point. On one occasion, a client called me from her ninety-four-year-old mother's house. The client went to stay with her for a few days because she (the client) had just called in hospice, and she wanted to help set it up and make sure everything was in order. While she was at her mother's desk, she noticed a delinquency notice from an insurance company for a $1,000,000 policy in a trust. It was for $10,000.

When she asked her mother why she hadn't paid the bill, her mother said it was too much money and told the trustee at the bank she didn't want to pay anymore! My client then called me and asked me what she should do. I immediately told her to call the company and make sure there was still time left in the grace period. Thank goodness, there was still ten days. I had her write a check as power of attorney and send the check and the copy of the power of attorney to the insurance company by overnight mail with signature required. Then, I had her call the next day to confirm receipt and acceptance of the check. Her mother died fewer than two months later. That was a case of right time, right place, right information.

Our best relationships are with clients who are up front about the details of their lives—and what they want for the future. Because the more information we have, the more we can do to help them live the life they want.

Lesson #5

A Financial Planning Relationship Is a Two-Way Street. It Thrives When There Is Mutual Respect

Finding ideal clients and establishing a two-way relationship with them is vital. We have had many clients over the years who have just needed to feel comfortable with us and our message before they trusted us completely. They've become good clients and friends. They've followed our advice, and we've been able to help them achieve their goals. That's all because we took the time to establish a relationship of mutual respect.

In the end, the clients who are a good match for us are truly looking for help. They want to be part of the process but realize they need professional help. They view money as important to living the life they want, not just as a game in which whoever accumulates the most wins. Most of our clients have a fairly high net worth. They could be corporate executives with big incomes and complicated benefit plans or simply folks who have worked hard over twenty- or thirty-plus years to accumulate a significant retirement nest egg in 401(k), 403(b), or 457 plans. In both cases, they're looking at retirement and how they will live the life they've been dreaming of.

More and more, we also have to consider multiple generations. Our clients may have older parents who require their care, adult children who rely on them for financial support, or grandchildren who need assistance. We take the time to understand the dynamics of all these relationships.

When I sit down with a prospective client, I consider their goals and explore all options and possibilities. How can I make this meeting valuable to them? What can I do to help them leave feeling as though they've learned something, that their time has been well spent? How can I plant a seed to give them greater confidence in their financial future?

I'm immensely proud of what we do, so I'd like to think everyone would desire to become a client immediately. However, we must be an ideal fit for each other. If we're fortunate, we will work with our clients for many decades and across multiple generations, so it helps to have a strong and healthy relationship from the start. Trust is key to any strong and lasting relationship, but we all know trust needs to be *gained over time.*

It often takes two or three years for us to develop a real, trusting client relationship, even after we start working together. Sometimes we click with clients much sooner, especially with referrals. Most of the time, however, we spend weeks and months working to establish trust so that our clients will continue to work with us long term and so that they will know we respect and understand them. After two or three years of meetings, client events, and communications—as well as monthly conference calls and other special client events and activities—we've built up a solid relationship of trust with our clients. They see us as friends.

We see them as friends. We can then continue to help them focus on their life goals, not just their money.

Building this kind of relationship often depends on the outcome of our initial meeting together. My job during that first meeting is to determine whether we have grounds for a good start. We realize a potential client may be skeptical. After all, there are too many horror stories of unscrupulous advisors taking advantage of investors, so they may be wondering, "What is she trying to sell me?" and "I'm not going to let her talk me into anything."

They may have worked with an advisor who put themselves first instead of mutually committing to a well-grounded financial planning relationship. That's what we look for: a mutual commitment. We need to cut through any ill-conceived notions of what it means to have a successful relationship with a truly professional financial advisor.

We've had more than a few people come into our offices after being referred by a current client and say, "Sign me up. I've heard so much about you. I just want to get started." Yet much more often, they come with a wall up. They're wary and admit, "My friend told me how wonderful you are, and she loves you, but . . ."

This is the trust-building stage. We love it when a potential client has a ton of questions. We try to answer them before they're even asked, and we're ready to answer many we may have never heard before. I ask potential clients, "Who are you, why are you here, and what would you like us to accomplish together?"

We carefully review the data form they filled out before the meeting so we can gain an understanding of their current situation. Sometimes, fact-finding can be tedious, but we try to make is as painless as possible. After all, top doctors don't make diagnoses without asking all the right questions.

Then we try to propose some quick and easy actions for them to take. That way we know we are delivering actual value from the outset. For us, it's important every potential client we meet feels that even just coming in for a complimentary meeting was a valuable experience. We try to deliver value every time we interact with a client.

Choosing the Right Business Partner

Choosing the right clients is truly important in a business like Eastern Planning. However, as you've seen from our history, choosing the right partner can make or break a business. Matthew has been a spectacular business partner for me. It's not just that he's my son (though that doesn't hurt a bit); it's how we complement each other and share the same philosophies about financial planning.

People wonder how my and Matthew's roles differ and why. Well, you can't do everything—you can only be good at what you're good at. I often joke that I can't do investments well because I have too much heart. Matthew has the brain and the analytical mind, and he can be unemotional when it comes to investing. If a client called me up and said, "Why aren't we selling!?" I'd probably just say, "Yeah, maybe we should!" But our differing skill sets complement each other and benefit our business and our clients.

Even though Matthew didn't formally join Eastern Planning until 2001 and become a partner until 2006, he's been working with me from the very beginning. When I started Eastern Planning in 1995, my children were teenagers. We held seminars with clients, and my children's job was not only to attend but to register the participants, hand out their books, and then sit with us and do their homework. That was their job! Then, at the end of the day, Matthew and Jacklyn (or some of their friends) would collect everything, say goodbye to people, do whatever else they had to do, and then we would all go home.

We would have seminars twice a week, so two nights they would go to seminars. Now, my son played football and wrestled, so of course we made some allowances for those activities. Otherwise, Matthew's job was right there alongside me. He and his sister ideally attended workshops for four years. Later, when Matthew attended college, he continued to come! Whenever he had a break, if we had a business trip, he would go with us—to be part of the education, not to see the sights or travel the world. He would even go to the conferences with us, and he was wholeheartedly involved. Back then, we were in a study group, and they used to call him "College Boy." "Is College Boy coming?" they'd ask, and College Boy was always there unless he was, you know, actually attending classes.

All of that meant Matthew was very well prepared to join Eastern Planning after he graduated, fully licensed, from Penn State with a business degree. After joining us, he also started on his Certified Financial Planner certification, which he quickly achieved. Unbeknownst to us, lurking ahead was a time when we needed strong, rational heads, and he definitely had one. As I wrote already, our business was quickly challenged by the

9/11 tragedy and its aftermath. Still, we stayed the course, and with Matthew's cool head, we came out stronger than ever. As Matthew's wrestling coach always told him, what doesn't kill you makes you stronger.

To make us an even a stronger team, Matthew continued to improve his investment knowledge. Immediately after joining Eastern Planning, Matthew studied hard and passed his CFP exam, then enrolled in the CFA program to become a Chartered Financial Analyst (which he completed in under three years). That wasn't enough for him; he then applied and enrolled in Columbia University's MBA program. In fewer than two years, through hard work and studying through the summer while working full-time, Matthew achieved an incredibly hard-earned MBA. What's more, he did this in 2007 and 2008, taking as many night courses as he could so he could be in-office during the day to support all the clients during the Great Recession.

Matthew and I make such a perfect team. And while I joke that I have too much heart to handle investing, I don't mean to imply that he doesn't have a heart—because he really does. He's a very mushy guy, but at work, he can analyze, he can categorize, and he can be calm and consistent, which is the most important part of investments. It's not just selecting the right investments; it's handling your emotions, and he can do that. He can help keep people from making emotional decisions. Behavioral management is a big, important piece of investing! Also, he's a true fiduciary. He is absolutely for the client first, and he is totally on top of it. He does all the research, making sure he's doing the best for every client.

Matthew also understands what doing the best for every client really means. He works to keep people consistent and true to their goals and objectives. Many times, people try to run after returns, chasing a big windfall or an exciting payout. Everybody wants to hit the home run. On the other side of things, when business and finance take a dive, everybody wants to jump ship. Whether the market is high or low, people often want to follow a path that will ultimately take them off the course toward their real goals. Matthew understands this and takes it into account to help steer our clients toward lasting, meaningful success long term—focusing on life, not just money.

In 2008, Matthew started hosting what he called fireside chats (because he loves history and remembered that FDR held fireside chats) to educate clients and to allow them to ask questions. He taught clients how to ride out the highs and lows of investing, reminding them that, with our approach and Matthew's keen insight and steady hand, we're not going to hit the home runs, but we probably won't strike out as much, and we're going to be consistent. As I mentioned, whether the market is high or low, people tend to want to jump—they can be just as volatile as the market itself! It's amazing how important it is be calm, and Matthew is good at helping people stay the course. His fireside chats helped our clients understand this frame of mind and see the bigger picture at hand.

Matt's fireside chats also demonstrated why good financial planning isn't just about setting up a plan or moving money around. It's also about holding hands and setting up cash flow that will see clients over a low spot in the market. We brought back fireside chats in 2020 during the coronavirus pandemic. Again, Matthew brought consistency and common sense to help our clients get through another crisis.

While I don't have the temperament to manage investments, Matthew doesn't have the time to spend developing expertise in retirement planning, Social Security, Medicare, and other financial planning strategies I focus on. Yet we complement each other well, and much of our success is because we trust each other.

Some clients lean more toward me because I'm down to earth and I don't talk in financial lingo. Matthew can communicate the intricacies and depth of investments, whereas I can bring it down to basics. Some clients don't understand it or don't *want* to understand it. However, on the other side, some of our clients love it! Those clients tend to gravitate a little more toward Matthew, and it works out really well.

One of the most important things for Matthew is to make sure our clients get the best investments for the least cost. He is always looking at the internal costs of the investment and making sure our clients receive value equal to those costs. He also likes to sit down with clients and explain all the hidden costs of an investment with them. When Matthew puts together a portfolio, you know he put serious thought into what he selected. It's never just one from column A and two from column B.

Of course, Matthew's work is not all about picking investments either. When he sits down with clients, he also listens to their stories and tries to understand who they are, what they want, and where they're hoping to go long term—all the important aspects of their lives. When he meets with a client who wants to set up a portfolio for retirement, for example, it's important for him to know they have a daughter in a "bad marriage" with a lot of debt, because the client worries that they will have to help or support their daughter. Information of that nature helps Matthew truly address clients' needs. In this situation, for example, he knows that they have a need for extra cash flow in case their daughter's situation requires it. He also recognizes that an overly aggressive portfolio might not work for them, even when they're highly tolerant of risk. This information about clients' lives is therefore essential for Matthew's aspect of our business as well, which is why he discusses many options with them whenever they meet.

I'm immensely grateful to share leadership of Eastern Planning with Matthew. Our partnership itself is an outstanding example of "It's not just money; it's life." He agreed with me about the direction Eastern Planning needed to take, and he saw what a challenging spot I was in, trying to rebuild the business. His choice to come and build it with me as opposed to joining a Wall Street firm is an affirmation of valuing life over money. His support and his moral compass have helped me stay focused on that vision through some hard times.

∾ Choosing the Right Team ∾

Eastern Planning wouldn't be the business it is today without our clients, Matthew, and our team. In our office, I believe we should treat each other the same way we treat our clients. There are too many toxic work environments out there and not enough supportive ones. If we want to provide world-class service to our clients, we have to start with how we treat our employees and how we work together.

I try to teach my staff that we're in it together. We would never say, "You only have five sick days left. That's it; too bad." We don't have that kind of philosophy in our office. I need help, they need help, and we need to work together. Their job is just as important as my job, because without them, I wouldn't be able to do my job.

I learned a concept a while ago about hats. Everybody has one—a fireman has a hat, a mother has a hat, an executive has a hat. Everyone wears many different hats in their life, but here at the office, we have a procedure guide for every hat, and it tells you what you do every day. It has enough detail so that if you can't come in some day, someone else can wear your hat seamlessly.

We have a contact management system, a software program that holds all this information, and each person's responsibilities are in the contact management system. It says once a month you do this, and once a week you do that, and here's what you do daily. How to do that chore is in the procedure manual on their desk. Here's when we water the plants; here's who turns on the copy machine daily; and here's how to check for birthday calls or write a postcard. Anybody can step in for everybody else—because we're a team.

Likewise, we're there for each other because we're a team. One of my team members has a young son. It works best for her if she can work from home one day a week, so she works from home one day a week. I'm not a very big stickler about sick days and personal days. Last year, unfortunately, a team member's husband ended up in the hospital with a major heart problem, and she was out for a good ten days. She did whatever she could to keep up. She came in early to do a little work or worked from home when she could. Then the rest of us did whatever we could to support her and maintain her job because that's the philosophy.

Our culture is, "I know you're not going to take advantage of me, and I'm not going to take advantage of you. We are here for each other." With this approach to our relationships, it's only natural to treat our clients this way too. Because it's not their money; it's their lives. That goes for everyone we work with, and it's a philosophy that has led to a great deal of happiness and success for everyone involved.

Lesson #6

Fiduciaries Are the Best Choice to Manage Your Aspirations

When I revamped Eastern Planning, I wasn't just trying to present another financial planning business to the world. I wanted the freedom to care deeply about people and their lives, deliver holistic financial planning, and provide exceptional experience to our clients. Your relationship with your financial planners should be enjoyable. The service we give our clients is important because they invest their time as well as their money when they work with us.

Our clients are looking for a true fiduciary, an advisor and an advisory firm that is always looking out for their best interests. We always do our best to help our clients invest without bias toward any particular financial product or toward how much money we may make by serving them. We help them understand all the costs related to their investments so they can make informed decisions. Yet, as I have already said many times, it's not just about investments. To be sure our clients are on the right track, we help them review their other financial relationships. We consider things like banking, insurance, and mortgages. For example, sometimes people come in and are overinsured or have too much of one kind of insurance and not enough of another. We help them review their options, whether or not we can directly help them make changes. We recommend what's in the client's best interests, period, and the client decides.

That's why we adopted the motto, "It's not just your money; it's your life"—and over the years, I've come to understand that it's *my* life too! When faced with the challenge of reimagining and rebuilding Eastern Planning, I realized I wanted my work to be supportive and helpful toward my other life goals. I wanted my focus to be about my own life, not just my money. I needed a business model and a client base that would allow me to live my life to the fullest. This goal has required constant adjustments and tweaks, like any good plan, but our approach to establishing trust and care with our clients has definitely gone both ways.

I've developed my business so that I can help support my daughter and my other family members and friends in whatever way necessary. If my daughter or daughter-in-law says to me, "One of my kids is sick, and neither one of us can stay home because we're both scheduled"—meaning she and her husband are both busy with work and they need some help with my grandson—well, my clients understand I'm a grandmother first! My ideal client is *not* someone who says, "Wait a second, we have an appointment. I don't care whether your grandson is sick." If I heard that from a client, my answer would be, "Well, then, I don't care to be involved in business with you. Goodbye."

Of course, I wouldn't say that outright to anyone, but I mean the sentiment behind those words. *It's not just money; it's life.* It's their life and my life both. Because my ideal clients and I have established a strong, positive relationship, they trust me enough to let me live my life. As a result, they know I work that much harder for them to enjoy *their* life, and that's the truest example I know of how, at Eastern Planning, we consider our clients family—and vice versa.

Having that kind of relationship with my clients is such a blessing, and it is exactly the outcome our tagline is meant to produce. It works both ways! If I said my mother wasn't feeling well and I had to go to her home in Florida to be with her, any client of mine would immediately urge me to do so and would ask what they could do to help. That's because we've shown them in our work that we're focused on *them*, not just their money, and they offer us the same consideration.

It's not just me, either. Everyone at Eastern Planning feels the same about our clients. For example, my son isn't a typical nine-to-five worker. A few times a week, he goes home in the afternoon to take his daughter from the bus and spend the afternoon with her. He gets to spend quality time with her and take her to karate and whatever else is going on in her life. Then he goes back to work at 8:00 at night. Sometimes he's writing emails at midnight! Still, he doesn't mind that one bit because he got to be home at 3:00 p.m. to be with his daughter. That's how we live our lives, and that's what allows us the opportunity to offer the same freedom to our clients.

That kind of business relationship we enjoy with our clients doesn't happen all at once, of course. Just like any long-term relationship, we get to know them a little at a time. As we meet and spend more time with them, we constantly learn new things by sharing experiences and history.

We start by listening to what a new client most wants to work on and tackling that first. We do that through more than just conversations; we also get to know them through client surveys.

An example of that follows:

1. What kind of books do you read?
2. What hobbies do you have?
3. What is your favorite snack?

We ask these kinds of questions and keep track of what we learn because it makes them believe we care—and we do. It's not just investing their money properly and getting their will set up. It's learning about them, their children, their grandchildren (if they have grandchildren), and how they feel about their children's college education—all of those things. We gradually put together a picture of our client's identity so we can help them throughout their life. If we can understand who they are, we understand what they're trying to achieve in their life and how their money can help them do that.

For instance, say we are working on their budget. We ask a lot of questions that aren't just about how they spend their money. In response to our questions, they say, "I love to go to my kid's soccer games." That tells us they're very family oriented. Maybe they mention their house at the seashore. They say, "When I go there, it's family time, and I don't get much family time because of my business travel." We learn they travel a lot for work and that family time is important to them. Five years from now, if they have a cash flow problem, we will never say to them, "Hey, maybe we should sell the shore house." Because it's not just the money, it's their life, and in this case, it's about how important family time is to them. We make certain they will have those assets regardless of the situation. Everything you can learn about your client helps you support them in living the life they want.

⌒ Caring about People ⌒

One of my goals for my staff is to find random acts of kindness to do for our clients, something we do just because. One time, a member of my team was talking to a client and found out that while on an international business trip, the client had a dental emergency. That afternoon we sent her a travel dental kit. It didn't help her with her dental emergency, but at least she knew we listened, and we cared.

If we make a call just to say hello and find out someone's grandson just graduated college, then we'll send him a book about managing his finances. It's just little things that make us all feel good and make our clients feel good. It's one way to get our staff involved in my clients' lives, because if we're looking for an idea for a random act of kindness, we have to ask questions to find out what's going on. It's part of us getting to know the real person.

For instance, we ask crazy questions like, "What do you like to read?" It is not a question most financial planners have on their intake form, but we want to know who you are. That particular question even generated an event! We realized we had a lot of clients who liked mysteries, so we hosted a murder mystery party where somebody "dies," and you form teams to solve the mystery. It turned out to be one of our biggest successes, and it came from my incredible assistant realizing that we had a lot of clients who liked mystery novels.

Those minor questions get combined with big questions—like, "If we felt something was wrong, who would you feel comfortable having us call?" Not "Who is your power of attorney?", because that's a different issue altogether. We need someone we can call and say, "Listen, my client said if we ever noticed something we're concerned about, we have permission to call you." I've had clients who started spending money in scary ways, and it was the first warning signal that something was happening for them. We don't just write it down and forget it. We act on it and call a loved one to talk about it.

We also want to be there for our clients when a spouse or loved one dies. We have a checklist of what to do: send a card, make sure we call to check on the client, and so forth. We also have a booklet to help them cope and understand the complicated financial nuances of a loved one's death. It lists all the practical things they may have to take care of. For instance, what to do with a car, how to change a will, or a reminder to check beneficiary designations—all the things clients aren't thinking about when they've lost someone. We've made this into our responsibility, because we do care about our clients as people, not just sources of work and income for us. We've become good friends with them, we care about them, and we are poised to help when uncertain times strike—and we do.

∾ We Want Raving Fans ∾

I make all my team members read *Raving Fans* by Kenneth Blanchard. *Raving Fans* is a phenomenal book that reminds us that we don't want clients—we want fans who go out and rave about us!

I try to instill in my team that clients are *not* interrupting us; they *are* us. When we serve them, we must always remember that we do what we do all the time. But this may be the first time the client has ever been in this situation. So we need to think about the little stuff:

- We must fill out forms correctly. There is no reason to ask them to do the same things over and over again.
- We must know whether they prefer coffee or tea when they meet with us—without asking. That helps them feel like they're part of the family.
- We must answer the phone with the correct attitude. They should never feel afraid to call us and ask questions.
- We must treat each other right. People enjoy working with a team that works well together.

When a client calls and interrupts your task, you must take a deep breath, smile, and answer the phone because we *want* that phone call. They understand that *clients* pay their salary, not Eastern Planning.

After all, as a fiduciary, we work for our clients. And everyone benefits when we truly know them, their families, their needs, and their lives. Because in the end, what we do is more than just knowing who our clients are—it's letting them know that they are part of the Eastern Planning family and that we want to take care of them.

Lesson #7

Don't Confuse
Investment Performance
with Planning Success

One of the greatest tragedies on Wall Street over the past thirty years has been the overemphasis on investment performance. Investors are constantly being told to measure the movement of their accounts, up or down, against an index like the S&P 500. Don't get me wrong—there is a time and place for this type of comparison. However, if someone comes to me and says, "Here's one account, a slice of my investment money, show me what you can do and I might give you more," I won't do it. Matthew covers this information when he meets with them, but I don't address it in our first meeting. We talk about planning, life goals, and objectives; we don't talk about investments.

For those who immediately want to dive into investment discussions, I tell them, "I'm sure there are plenty of people who could do a good job managing this money if all you want to do is measure investment performance, and you should go find them. We have found that chasing returns is a fool's game. It takes your eye off the ball of achieving your ultimate goals. It may even mean you end up taking on more risk in your portfolio than you need. We need to see and understand the entire picture, not just one account. We want to help you reach your objectives, not feel good because your account was up a bunch this quarter. We want you to live the life you want to live and not feel like you have to worry about the ups and downs of the stock market month-in and month-out. We can't do that unless we can grasp who you are and what you want and review your total financial situation."

This doesn't mean we have to manage all of a new client's assets all at once, but we have to be given the opportunity to understand the whole of who that family is and know where all their assets are held and how they're being invested. We need to develop a holistic plan that reflects risk and reward parameters.

For example, in 2007 we got a new client from a referral. They were rather conservative, and two firms managed their money. One firm had their accounts in a mostly equity portfolio and the other, a family friend, had mostly high-quality bonds. They decided to move the equity portfolio over to us and, for the time being, leave the bond portfolio with their family friend. Remember, this was 2007. Matthew realized they were really quite risk adverse, and put the equity portfolio into a well-balanced, diversified portfolio. I did a comprehensive plan with them and went over budgeting, monthly distributions, estate planning, reviewed insurance, etc. However, during 2008 they called Matthew up in a panic.

What was happening to their other portfolio? It was going down more than the one my son was managing. Matthew immediately asked for a copy of their most recent statement— and somehow, between the time he saw the statement in 2007 until the middle of the downturn of 2008, someone had moved the account from corporate bonds to a large selection of bank stocks! That is why it is so important for us to know the complete picture. Remember, we do not just manage money. We walk beside our clients through a lifetime of dreams, aspirations, and accomplishments.

In our early years, we had investors come to us to execute trades. They really just wanted a stockbroker. We decided not to be in that business, as operating that way would not allow us to truly help our clients make smart decisions. The same is true today with the onslaught of do-it-yourself and day trading services. Investors who prefer to manage their money on their own by constantly staying plugged into the financial markets are not a good fit.

We operate as a partner with our clients by helping them make intelligent, well-informed decisions. As we develop financial plans, we give them options and choices that are based on our understanding of their greatest goals. We never dictate to them what they have to do by plugging them into a cookie cutter portfolio. No two investors are exactly the same. We attract people who understand our philosophy of open, honest, and ongoing dialogue. That's why our clients don't typically work with more than one advisor. We become their sole source of ongoing financial and life planning advice.

Quite often, we have to educate the people we meet on what it means to have a financial plan. A lot of folks have preconceived notions of planning as a tool that only helps achieve a single goal. They want us to look at one aspect of their life and not another. They only want to focus on college planning, retirement planning, estate planning, or investment planning. Those clients don't see how each of these planning topics are interrelated and need to be viewed together.

Or worse, some couples do not come to us as couples. Sometimes only one spouse wants to be in charge of the finances.

In this case, we tell them how important it is for the nonfinancial spouse to be involved in the planning. They do not have to make the decisions, but they must understand what is happening and why. Many times, when the financial spouse dies, the nonfinancial spouse is totally unprepared to carry on. Plus, as the advisor, we wouldn't know who they are or what their goals and objectives are, nor how their personal wishes match up with those of their partner. If both partners in a relationship are not willing to be at least partially involved in the planning process, we do not generally take them on as a client.

We love our clients, so one thing we don't like to do is fire them. However, we can only work with clients who respect us individually and as a team. I fired a client because she was always really nice when she spoke with me or Matt, but she abused the rest of my team. When her name showed up on the phone, the staff would fight over who would have to answer it—and not in a good way. This was upsetting to my staff and both Matt and me. Frequently, I told her how my staff felt and asked her to treat them with respect. Unfortunately, she could not adhere to my wishes. After a few more attempts, she forced me to ask her to transfer her accounts. We need to have trust, honesty, and respect. It's our culture—a culture of family. We're all here to help one another.

Again, we love our clients. We never want to fire them, and we normally don't! We have excellent retention with our client base, but sometimes we find our clients aren't a good fit with our philosophy and approach. For instance, every so often we have clients who panic sell or performance chase. Recently, we had a client whose new husband became involved with the financial planning and ended up selling at the absolute low for the month. He did this out of panic. He saw the markets dropping and worried that our plan would not work.

We had several conversations about investments with the client in question. Every time, we told her what would likely happen, and we explained it would be very difficult for her to get back in once she got out completely. We advised her not to sell. In the end, even though she wanted to remain a client, we had to tell her it wasn't a good fit. We felt she didn't mesh well with our strategy, and we wouldn't be able to properly help her with her needs moving forward, so we moved her account out and found her someone else to work with.

We also had another client recently who was a big performance chaser. This is a fairly common impulse, but it's one we discourage with our clients. We're focused on long-term planning, after all. We want them to look at the big picture and stay away from more momentary or fleeting opportunities that won't help them in the long run.

Of course, sometimes they insist on chasing big performance anyway. This client insisted on always being in the "hot thing" of the day. Matthew spoke to this client almost every month. Every time, Matthew would contemplate letting the client go, but then the client would seem to listen, and Matthew would think we could maybe continue to work together well. On and on it went, but the client still wanted to chase big performances and run things counter to our entire philosophy. In the end, we told him the same thing—it wasn't a good fit—and helped him move his accounts elsewhere.

⟜ Our Approach to Investments ⟞

Once I meet with clients and get a sense of the person's whole situation, I explain to them who we are at Eastern Planning, what we do, how we do it, and how we can help them accomplish their goals. I go through a few situations with them, and I try to find solutions that differ from those they've heard in the past. My clients don't come to me for the same old solutions—they need something that works. During this process, their skepticism decreases. If I've done my job well, they become hopeful.

The last step in my first meeting is letting them know that if this is something they're interested in, they can meet Matthew, my business partner, my son, and Eastern Planning's Chief Investment Officer. He explains what we invest in, how we invest, the fee schedule, risk tolerance, our investment philosophy—all the details. He gives them examples of the types of investments we use. They still don't have to make a commitment; the meeting with Matthew remains complimentary. After that meeting, they go home again, think about what Matthew and I have had to say, and decide.

⟜ First Steps for New Clients ⟞

When prospective clients come back and they're ready to commit, we have what we call a Mutual Commitment Meeting. Matthew usually leads this conversation. The first thing they do is decide on an investment policy statement that takes goals, risk tolerance, and other personal circumstances into consideration.

Everything we've learned about them goes into shaping their investment policy.

This meeting can be very intense, and we dive into a lot of details. Especially at the beginning of our client relationship, if our client asks, "What have you been doing lately?" our answer would be, "Everything!" When you're initiating a new financial planning relationship, we can't take anything for granted. We don't want to leave anything out. Each decision they have made to date needs to be viewed in the light of their new plan.

Most new clients come to us with a preexisting portfolio of investments. Now, Matthew can look at their investments and say, "Oh well, all of these things are okay, but they don't match what you need to make your plan work for the long run, so let's sell everything right away and put it into a model portfolio."

In reality, we could make our jobs easier if we just used the same models for everyone. And many advisors do just that. But is that in the best interests of our clients? No way.

As I mentioned previously, 9/11 had a major impact on us, both professionally and personally. But it also shaped Matthew's approach to investing. When he graduated and joined Eastern Planning in June 2001, he was excited to jump into a business that needed his expertise. Then came 9/11, and it was all hands on deck. How could we keep our clients afloat?

That was when he realized it was not just about investing; it was about people and their lives and circumstances. What we did mattered. Their lives were in our hands. His philosophy molded into making sure clients were well-balanced. It was not about hitting home runs. It's like the children's story, "The Tortoise and the Hare." We could put together an exciting portfolio full of opportunities, but if those options didn't pan out, what would happen to our client's retirement, their life?

In designing an investment policy, Matthew looks at several things, including tax consequences. He learns the client's history and preferences—for example, sometimes clients have stock from the corporation they worked for their entire life, or they don't want to sell the stock their mother left them. Every situation is unique, and he takes the time to learn about the client in order to cater to their different needs. After all those conversations and research, some things are kept, others are sold, and we postpone several decisions for the best interests of the client. We don't just take the portfolio and say, "Oh, you fit into option #2, and option #2 looks like this." Building an investment portfolio should not be like choosing a meal from a fast-food menu. Like fine dining, you may need to make changes that will truly satisfy your diet and appetite.

Matthew puts together a proposal for this meeting based on what we've learned from the clients themselves. After transferring accounts over, he focuses on rebalancing their finances, setting up beneficiary designations, and taking care of the other initial tasks he's identified to best benefit them. He keeps a careful eye on taxes and other fees involved to make sure the clients are making the best use of their money.

Next, Matthew explains and moves forward with the buckets paradigm of savings—which I'll explain shortly—followed by tax planning, investments, and other topics. This meeting is another chance for us to become familiar with the clients' desires and goals. By this point, we've found people who *want* us to help them with their financial lives—clients who aren't focused on short-term reforms but trust us to handle their long-term plan effectively.

It's important that we help them handle non-investor issues in order to benefit the rest of their family and their lives.

Matthew's Mutual Commitment Meeting with the clients provides the perfect opportunity to get the ball rolling on their investment and other financial plans that will benefit them over the rest of their lives.

after they found out their daughter's husband died without insurance. The only option they found feasible was having their daughter and two young children move in with them. It was a workable solution but was going to impair their retirement severely. What if that son-in-law had gotten life insurance?

Revisiting different topics at different times throughout the years keep our clients' financial plans fresh. Sometimes clients come in with something they want to talk about—their daughter's getting married, they're having a grandchild, they got a scary diagnosis. These topics and more are crucial to their financial well-being. Without listening to all their concerns, we would have no way to help anyone achieve their goals.

Personal circumstances affect our financial decisions. Period. Therefore emergencies, medical expenses, and anything involving family provides clients with a greater sense of urgency, and we need to stay on top of clients' financial plans.

Say I meet with a client and find out his sixty-nine-year-old wife was just diagnosed with Alzheimer's (which has happened). Fortunately, when they first started financial planning, part of what they did was buy excellent long-term care insurance.

When a client receives a diagnosis like this, various things need to happen. First, I find out what is necessary to file a claim. Next, we look at their legal documents. We set up a meeting with their attorney to work through the issues of health care proxies, the durable power of attorney, beneficiary designations, and so forth. Then we sit down with the family to speak with them about the long-term plan and their newfound responsibilities. These can be complicated steps, and clients are rarely in the right frame of mind to remember everything or figure it out on their own. That's why their relationship with us is pivotal and why knowing their whole situation and goals is so valuable on our end. The more we know, the better we can respond to bad news and changing circumstances.

Through it all, we always focus on providing our clients with the best outcomes for their *life*, not just their money. That's why things like buying long-term care insurance are such vital decisions. When you're in a serious situation, running out of money is not an option. It is extremely sad when a couple retires with no financial burdens and their dreams in front of them, but then the unexpected stops them short. At the very least, they do not have to worry about how to pay for the care. No matter the complications, we make sure they're taken care of.

Life happens. Changes have to happen, and that's why it's important to stay in touch, know what's going on, and keep everything up to date. We need to be able to respond to what's going on for our clients.

Lesson #9

A Well-Designed Financial Plan Will Help You Make Decisions about More Than Just Your Financial Assets

When I meet with clients, I can listen between the lines and hear when something might need to change. The other day, I was listening to a client who is unhappy at work. She's not a spender, so she has put away an enormous amount of money.

"Would you quit if you could?" I asked, and her eyes widened. As it turned out, the only thing holding her back was making sure she could cover medical insurance. We sorted that out, and now I'm helping her retire well before she thought she should because she can. Of course, there are people who work well past when they can retire because they love working, but there are others who come to me miserable. When they discover, "I can live on this now?!", they're like, "The next time my boss yells at me, I am out of there!" That doesn't mean they go in and quit, but it means they know they can if they desire to. That's the power of knowing what your money can do for your life.

❧ Caring about Good Planning ❧

We help clients live their best lives, but ironically, a big part of financial planning is planning for death. I remember one client who gave her daughter a lot of money. Her daughter was a professional who made bad choices and was consistently in financial crisis. I could not get the mother to stop giving her daughter money.

Ultimately, I told her she was going to run out of money, and she had to put herself first. However, with a mother's love, she couldn't do that. She assumed she would die young, as had happened with a streak of relatives. I warned her again that she was going to run out of money, but she wouldn't listen.

Betting that you are going to die young is not a financial plan for the future. Many people don't die young. Eventually, we got to the tipping point. If she didn't stop giving her daughter money, she was going to run out of money. I told her this and noted that she wasn't dead yet—perhaps she still had plenty of time left on the planet. Now? She's pinching every penny, but she didn't break herself. Some clients need permission to spend, while others need a reality check.

Good financial planning can afford a sense of peace and stability during difficult times, just as with our lovely client who got lung cancer and died way too early. Because of our planning, she had long-term care insurance. She was able to get the best care throughout her illness and not be a burden to her husband. He was given the opportunity to just be there for her. His future was protected by our work. Because we did the whole plan and asked all the tough questions, we set her up for both living and, unfortunately, for dying. Still, she died well.

People think they are protecting their families by setting specific beneficiaries to various accounts, but it can backfire. I worked with a family in which the father put his eight-year-old son down as a beneficiary on an annuity, planning to use it for his son's college expenses. In naming his son as the beneficiary, his intention was to protect his son in the future. Tragically, the father died from brain cancer before the son turned eighteen. The mother came to me at an attorney's referral because minors cannot be named as outright beneficiaries to inherit money. She had to become her son's guardian in court, and then she was very limited in how they could invest the money. When he became a teenager and wanted to spend that money, the court backed him up, and his mother couldn't stop him from using that college fund as he wanted.

Fortunately, it wasn't a large expense and there were still enough assets for him to attend a state college. Although, if somebody had said to the father, "This is what could happen if you put your son as the beneficiary," he probably wouldn't have done it. To give that kind of service, you have to know your client, understand their concerns and plans, and give them options and choices.

Sometimes it's a case of not knowing what you don't know. A woman came to me right after the SECURE Act was signed into law, which made it easier for small business owners to set up retirement plans that are less expensive and easier to administer. One part of that act specified that most IRA beneficiaries had to pull all the money out of the IRA within ten years. In our interview with the client, she told me her father had recently passed away. Since he died before the starting date of the act, she could still set up a decedent IRA and stretch the father's IRA over her lifetime. However, prior to meeting with me, she had signed the form from the annuity company for 100 percent distribution of the assets to be sent to her. It was $280,000. If hundreds of thousands of dollars were given to her outright, then hundreds of thousands of dollars of taxable income would have been added to her taxes that year—$65,000 or more! I told her no! We immediately put in a call to the compliance department of the investment company because she had already signed the forms. After moving up the ladder, we were able to cancel it in time and say it was because the adviser had given her bad advice. I explained the other options they had. She could not believe they would be able to save paying all that tax money. And at that time, we could stretch that IRA income over her entire life. She was only sixty-six at the time, so the income from this stretch IRA would add to her quality of life for a long time.

Although the SECURE Act took away the stretch IRA for many individuals, the act preserved it for others. For example, I have a client with three children, one of whom has special needs. Due to the SECURE Act, planning for a special needs child has completely changed. Before, we wouldn't have put the child's trust on the IRA beneficiary form, but now a Special Needs Trust is allowed to stretch the IRA instead of taking it out in ten years. This completely changed their current plan, which had listed the other two children as the beneficiaries of the IRA and listed the special needs child as the beneficiary of the life insurance policy. After the SECURE Act, we made the special needs trust the beneficiary of the IRA and the other two children the beneficiaries of the life insurance policy. This is a perfect example of why making a plan and putting it on a bookshelf doesn't work.

I have a very wealthy client who wants to give as much as she can spend to the charities she loves *now*, while she's alive. Her desire is not about maintaining her wealth. It's about maintaining enough wealth so that she can maintain her standard of living. It's not about keeping her principal; it's about her donating as much as she wants to donate.

I wouldn't know that if I didn't know her as a person. I might tell her, "No, you're giving away too much. You're not getting enough tax deductions." But she's not worried about tax deductions. She gets joy from giving away her money and seeing it do good in the world, so I support her. I make sure she has enough information to make excellent decisions, and I cheer her on.

A good financial professional should do the same by asking you questions like:

- Do you have legal documents?
- Who have you named in your legal documents?
- Is your relationship with that person intact?
- Who is in your beneficiary designations? Are they still appropriate?
- Do you have a power of attorney? Who is it?
- As you are getting older, who are we going to call if problems arise?

If they aren't asking you these types of questions, then it's just about your money, not your life.

Although managing money is a large part of what we do, our clients care most about what we do for their lives. They know that in investing, there's going to be some good years and some bad years, and they're not out chasing the best performance all the time, because that's not what life is about. What they care about is that we listen, we watch out for them, and they're not going to fall between the cracks. Because we've established that relationship of trust, they know that we'll keep them up to date about their finances and that we're prepared to help in any circumstance or need. That allows them a much greater degree of freedom and peace of mind.

Most of our new clients now are referrals. Word of mouth is by far our best promotion. I'm tremendously proud of that, because I think it reflects the culture we've built with our team and the care we give to serving clients.

Final Thoughts

I t's been over two decades since I developed and molded Eastern Planning into the business that I always wanted it to be. I've learned a lot in those years, and all that work has brought me to living a life I love. Before I wrap up this book, I want to revisit the nine lessons I learned along the way and share a couple of highlights of my career.

∿ My Nine Lessons ∿

1. A plan isn't a plan if you don't properly put it into action.
2. Good planning leads to a more enjoyable life.
3. No plan is perfect. Always be prepared to make difficult decisions.
4. Tell it all! Good planning starts with detailed information.
5. A financial planning relationship is a two-way street. It thrives when there is mutual respect.

6. Fiduciaries are the best choice to manage your aspirations.
7. Don't confuse investment performance with planning success.
8. Investment portfolios are unique to your circumstances, so don't just settle for predetermined models.
9. A well-designed financial plan will help you make decisions about more than just your financial assets.

These lessons have shaped me and everything I've worked to create. Looking back at when it all started—that day when I sat with Alan's client—I know my path wasn't always easy and that it may have cost me a lot personally. However, focusing on taking one step at a time, I can now say that what Matt and I have built is exactly the life and business I envisioned for myself.

ᘓ It Is *Not* Lonely at the Top ᘔ

Surrounding yourself with clients you love is one thing. Success, at that point, is a given. However, my team makes the business run like a sewing machine. I mentioned the hat concept above, and it is true: no matter who is wearing which hat, we know everyone can (and will) step in as necessary and use another hat when needed.

There is something to be said for being able to rely on those around you, and it is much rarer than you may first think. Finding incredible people to help you run a business like Eastern Planning is not only difficult but imperative. My team is the heart and soul of our firm, fueling it—by helping our clients—to keep our perfect motor running.

Additionally, professional friendships have encouraged Eastern Planning's expansion from the very beginning. I mentioned a friend who had separated from her business partnership to "go it on her own" around the same time I did. She was (and still is) indispensable to me and I to her. Therefore, success does not drive people from you; it only attracts incredible ones to you.

∿ Work with Women ∿

One of my great pleasures is mentoring young women entering financial planning. Things have changed a *lot* since 2001. When you consider the challenges of women in the workplace, you think back to the diversification and HR issues of the 1950s or 1960s. They had their challenges—but those challenges didn't go away. In fact, in 2001 many people scoffed at the idea of me running Eastern Planning on my own. While it was a sad situation, it didn't surprise me. That was how things were done nineteen years ago. Yes, it really has been that long.

Now, women are taking over the workplace. Young women who are entering financial planning need the support and guidance of people like me, who have been through some of the trials and errors of being a woman in what was once a male-dominated business sector. As this form of business continues to gradually welcome more and more women, I look forward to helping them find their place, just like I did.

Another great pleasure is the ability to do more pro bono work. That's something I couldn't imagine being able to afford back in 2001. I've started to work with more women to help get their finances under control. I can't help everyone that I might like to help, but I have several with whom I work regularly, including some young people I'm helping to get started on the right path.

I'm also working with one woman whose husband died in his early forties. He left her with no money. She doesn't have any children, but I want to get her to a point where she's not panicking about not being able to pay her bills. I feel blessed that the way we've built our business gives me the time to serve people in this fashion.

ᕙ Community—Not Just Clients ᕗ

When it comes down to it, the hard work and herculean effort the team of Eastern Planning puts in daily makes our clients' lives better. Yes, we do what we can for them financially, but it goes beyond that. For example, during the coronavirus pandemic of 2020, we knew many of our older clients were facing much time alone. We made it our job to call them up—and even Zoom them, if they were up to it—just to hear how they were doing. We started planning fun things they could do from home, like a bingo night and an Eastern Planning anniversary party (where we sent them big cookies with "25" written on them). We gave our clients a community, a place to belong.

Because no matter what we are facing, we are there for each other, and we are there for our clients. Because it isn't just their money.

It's their life.

Author Biography

Drawing upon her many years of experience in retirement planning and particular expertise in distribution strategies, Beth Blecker provides clients approaching their retirement years or in times of transition with proactive financial strategies. She understands that it's not just your money, it's your life, and she works toward helping others establish financial balance.

A long-time member of Ed Slott Master Elite Advisors, an organization of financial advisors dedicated to serving as leaders in the IRA industry, Beth teaches retirement planning and distribution strategies to local CPA groups and corporations, as well as at various financial services industry events.

Beth has long been involved in helping women develop financial literacy. She offers regular workshops and has hosted a weekly internet show, Taking Control: Financial Independence for Women (translated for the hearing-impaired). She is also past president of the Rockland Business Women's Network, a non-profit organization that supports and empowers women by providing networking and educational opportunities.

A graduate of Fairleigh Dickinson University, Beth helped launch Eastern Planning in 1995 after a twenty-year career in corporate and public accounting. In 2000, she took over as CEO and has grown Eastern Planning into a firm known for its personal, practical advice and superior client service.

Beth's passionate interest in her community has inspired her to volunteer in many areas. She has served on the board of People to People and the Holocaust Center and has been a Big Sister with the Rockland County Big Brothers Big Sisters program. She now continues to serve as a mentor.

An active tennis player, Beth also loves spending time with her young grandchildren, Reid, Spencer, Harrison, and Daniel.

~

I would appreciate your feedback on what chapters
helped you most, and what you would like
to see in future books.

If you enjoyed this book and found it helpful,
please leave a REVIEW on Amazon.

Visit us at www.EasternPlanning.com
where you can sign up for email updates.

Connect with me directly by email:
bblecker@easternplanning.com.

Thank you!